SUMMARY

Review & Analysis of

Diamandis and Kotler's Book

Bold

BusinessNews Publishing

BOOK PRESENTATION: *BOLD* BY PETER DIAMANDIS AND STEVEN KOTLER

BOOK ABSTRACT

MAIN IDEA

The world's biggest problems are today's biggest business opportunities. The key to success is to become an "exponential entrepreneur" – that is, an entrepreneur who harnesses the growing power of exponential technologies to best effect.

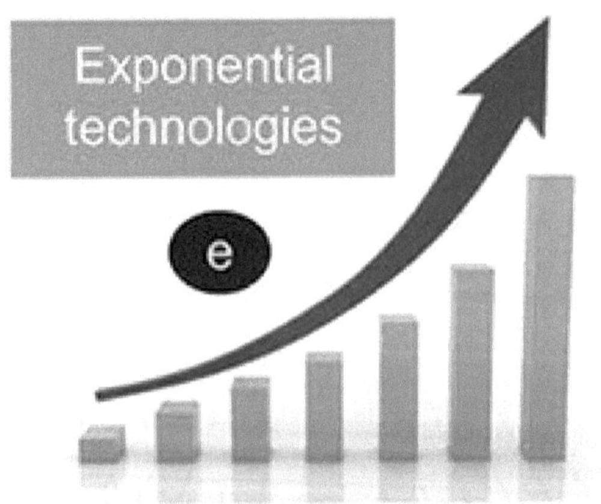

The world is now on an exponential growth curve. Technologies which double in power on a regular basis are showing up in dozens of arenas: networks, sensors, robotics, digital medicine and nanotechnology to name only a few. These technologies pave the way for an increasingly abundant future for the world but it's up to us to make the most of them. That's where exponential entrepreneurs have the chance to shine.

The power to tackle big challenges and make a difference has been democratized. Instead of being the exclusive realm of royalty, governments or multinationals, today anyone with an Internet connection or even a smartphone is in the game. If you have the passion, you can bring real change into the world – and benefit tremendously.

> *"While we truly believe that creating a world of abundance is possible, it is by no means guaranteed. Our deepest hope is that you will get inspired to get off the couch and change the world. When Steve Jobs said that the goal of every entrepreneur should be to 'put a dent in the universe' – he wasn't talking about inventing the next Angry Birds."*
>
> *– Peter Diamandis and Steven Kotler*
>
> *"Ultimately, the best way to become a billionaire is to solve a billion-person problem."*
>
> *– Peter Diamandis and Steven Kotler*

ABOUT THE AUTHOR

PETER DIAMANDIS is chairman and CEO of the X PRIZE Foundation, a nonprofit which offers large incentive prizes for radical technology breakthroughs. The Foundation is best known for the $10 million prize it offered for private spaceflight and the $10 million prize offered for cars which achieve 100 miles-per-gallon fuel efficiency. Dr. Diamandis is also co-founder and chairman of Singularity University, co-founder and vice-chairman of Human Longevity Inc. and co-founder and co-chairman of Planetary Resources. He and Steven Kotler co-authored *Abundance – The Future Is Better Than You Think*. He is a graduate of MIT and Harvard Medical School.

STEVEN KOTLER is a best-selling author and an award-winning journalist. His articles have appeared in 75 publications including *Wired, Popular Science, National Geographic* and the *New York Times Magazine*. He is the co-founder and director of research at the Flow Genome project. He writes a blog for *Forbes* about innovation (Far Frontiers) and another for *Psychology Today* (The Playing Field) about sport and culture. He is a graduate of the University of Wisconsin and the John Hopkins University.

The Web site for this book is at www.boldbook.com

IMPORTANT NOTE ABOUT THIS EBOOK

This is a summary and not a critique or a review of the book. It does not offer judgment or opinion on the content of the book. This summary may not be organized chapter-wise but is an overview of the main ideas, view points and arguments from the book as a whole. This means that the organization of this summary is not a representation of the book.

SUMMARY OF *BOLD* (PETER DIAMANDIS AND STEVEN KOTLER)

1. WHAT EXACTLY ARE EXPONENTIAL TECHNOLOGIES?

Exponential technologies are those which don't just grow in a linear fashion but keep on doubling over and over. Humans aren't very good at understanding exponentials because their growth is so small in the early stages that it looks like nothing is happening. However, thanks to computers, sensors and communication technology, we now live and work in an exponential world where amazing opportunities are poised to explode in the next three to five years.

Humans are pretty good at understanding linear growth:

1 ----▶ 2 ----▶ 3 ----▶ 4 ----▶ 5 ----▶ 6

We're much less adept, however, at understanding just how dramatic exponential growth can be:

1 ----▶ 2 ----▶ 4 ----▶ 8 ----▶ 16 ----▶ 32

To give an example, if you take 30 linear steps from your starting point, you end up about 30 meters or 90 feet away. By contrast, if you were to take 30 exponential steps from the same starting point, you would end up about one billion meters away – roughly the same distance as orbiting the Earth 26 times. The latter stages of any exponential sequence generate awe-inspiring growth.

The most widely known example of exponential growth is Moore's Law, coined by Intel founder Gordon Moore in 1965. He stated the number of integrated circuits on a transistor double every twelve to twenty-four months. Moore's Law has held for the last sixty years and is the underlying reason why a smartphone today is about a thousand times faster and a million times cheaper than a 1970s era supercomputer. This is a good example of exponential growth in action.

To avoid the easy-to-do pitfall of underestimating exponential growth, keep in mind a framework called "The Six Ds of Exponentials." It goes something like this:

- **D1** *Digitalization* – once a process transitions from physical to digital, exponential dynamics kick in
- **D2** *Deception* – the early stages of exponential growth often go unnoticed and is unremarkable
- **D3** *Disruption* – eventually new markets are created and existing markets are disrupted
- **D4** *Demonetization* – people stop buying the old technology and it basically becomes free
- **D5** *Dematerialization* – the technology becomes embedded in other products
- **D6** *Democratization* – objects are turned into bits and hosted on a digital platform for everyone

Digital cameras are the perfect example of this phenomena in action. In 1996, Kodak sold film and had 140,000 employees and $28 billion in market capitalization. Digital cameras first arrived in 1976 (D1) but didn't have enough resolution to be useful for twenty years (D2). However, once digital cameras passed the two million pixel barrier (D3), people stopped buying film (D4) and Kodak filed for Chapter 11 bankruptcy in January 2012. Once smartphones came to market, people stopped buying digital cameras (D5) because their smartphone had a high-quality multi-megapixel camera which came as part of the phone. Today, you can share photos for free (D6) with your friends on multiple online sites without using anything more than your smartphone.

While Kodak was riding the Six Ds of Exponentials to bankruptcy, other companies have harnessed the power of exponential technology to great effect. For example, Instagram started in October 2010 as a new platform for people to share photos online. When Instagram for Android was released in April 2012, it was downloaded more than a million times that first day. By the time Instagram had 30 million users, Facebook became concerned this photo-sharing service was becoming too much like a social network. Thus, on April 9, 2012, Facebook acquired Instagram for $1 billion. Instagram had gone from start-up to a billion-dollar valuation in eighteen months with only thirteen employees. That's the power of exponential platforms and organizations.

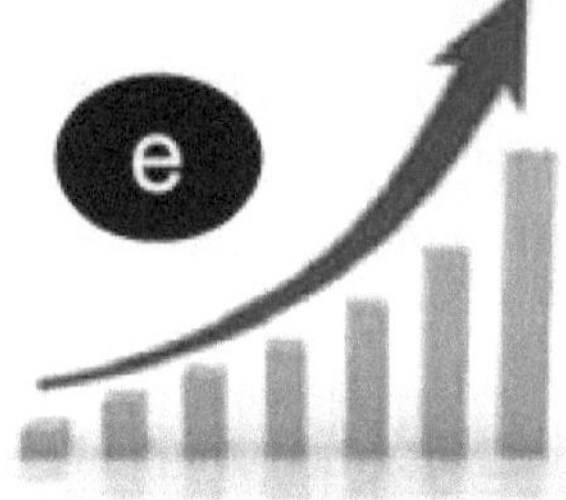

Another exponential technology which is coming to prominence today is additive manufacturing otherwise called 3-D printing. Traditional manufacturing is subtractive – you start with a block of material and take stuff away until you're left with the desired object. 3-D printing is additive – you build objects one layer of material at a time.

3-D printers have been under development for thirty years now and many of the pioneers in this field no longer exist. 3-D Systems, a Californian company, almost shut down as well but was finally able to bring to market 3-D printers which have found use in prototyping and localized manufacturing. Today, 3-D Systems is a thriving $6 billion company which sells more than forty different printers.

The largest of their printers is capable of printing a car dashboard as a single piece, their smallest machine is a home 3D printer called the Cube. Circa 2015, 3D printing is on the cusp of incredible exponential growth as more and more people get into this.

Additive digital manufacturing is poised to explode over the next five years. Made-to-order manufacturing will completely revolutionize several multi-trillion-dollar industries such as:

- Commercial aerospace and defense
- Space exploration
- Automotive manufacturing
- Health care
- Consumer products / retail

Note that most exponential technologies tend to follow a "Hype Curve" which looks something like this:

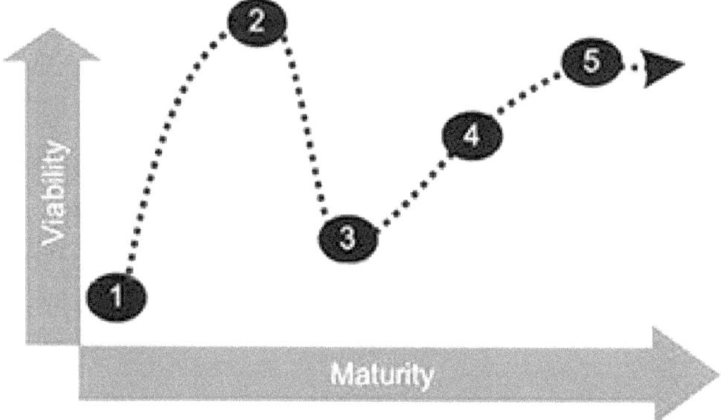

Point 1 is when some new technology comes along which has obvious potential. Everyone gets enthusiastic because they can envision the technology in its final form and there is a peak (point 2) of inflated expectations. Inevitably, the early prototypes disappoint which leads to a trough of disillusionment (point 3).

It's not unusual for exponential technologies to linger in that trough for many years while user interfaces are developed and while the technology gains more capabilities. Eventually, the technology moves up the slope of entitlement (point 4) and unleashes massive productivity (point 5) which transforms entire industries.

From an entrepreneurial perspective, the perfect time to get involved with an exponential technology is when it is just about to exit the trough and start up the slope of entitlement. The indicators of this transition include:

- Best practices get developed and entrenched
- There is a rapid proliferation of suppliers
- Secondary financing becomes available
- A simple and elegant user interface emerges

At the present time, there are five technologies which are primed for exponential growth in the very near future:

1. NETWORKS AND SENSORS

Today there are over seven billion smartphones in existence but within the next ten years, it is forecast there will be more than a trillion sensors hooked into the Internet. These sensors will provide real-time information and automation capabilities which will be reformational for many industries. The "Internet of Things" is poised for explosive growth in its reach and capabilities.

2. INFINITE COMPUTING

Computing is rapidly evolving from being a scarce resource into something that is plentiful and so cheap it becomes essentially free.

> *"By 2020, a chip with today's processing power will cost about a penny which is the cost of scrap paper."*
>
> *– Michio Kaku, theoretical physicist, CUNY*

> *"The cloud is democratizing our ability to leverage computing on a massive scale. We're entering an epic period of global innovation where high-performance computing is abundant, reliable and affordable."*
>
> *– Graham Weston, chairman and cofounder, Rackspace*

The opportunity here is everyone will have the ability to build their big idea atop an incredibly powerful infrastructure which is cheap, available on demand and unlimited. This will spur a period of global innovation which has never before been feasible.

3. ARTIFICIAL INTELLIGENCE

AI is finally poised to become completely ubiquitous in our daily lives. Today, 80 percent of jobs in the service industry can be broken down into four skills: looking, reading, writing and integrating knowledge. Computers can now outperform humans in all these skills and it all comes together in AI.

IBM has uploaded Watson (its AI supercomputer) to the cloud and made it available as a development platform to anyone who wants to use it. The applications are unlimited. A startup called Modernizing Medicine empowers any doctor who signs up to search millions of journal articles, textbooks, patient outcomes and scientific papers to develop individualized point-of-care information through an AI interface. That's just the tip of the iceberg.

4. ROBOTICS

iRobot now sells Baxter, a robot which is human safe. You program it by moving the robot's arms through the motions you want it to replicate. Soon, AI will mean you'll be able to program Baxter by having a conversation with it.

Baxter is the first robot you can build a business around – and it's just one of many next-generation robots now becoming available.

It has been suggested up to 45 percent of American jobs are at risk of being taken by robots within the next two decades. They will be pervasive and this presents an incredible entrepreneurial opportunity.

5. SYNTHETIC BIOLOGY

Synthetic biology is built around the idea that DNA is essentially software – a four-letter code arranged in a specific order. DNA instructs a cell to make specific proteins and such. Researchers can now swap nature's original DNA code with human-written code, thus programming the cell to produce whatever we specify.

While this sounds like the stuff of science fiction, synthetic biology is here already. It's really just a form of genetic engineering which has gone digital. You can use synthetic biology to make new fuels, foods, medicines, construction materials, clothing fibers and even new organisms in the lab rather than with industrial processes. Bioengineering is just about to become an entrepreneurial playground of historic proportions.

2. WHAT IS THE BOLD MINDSET?

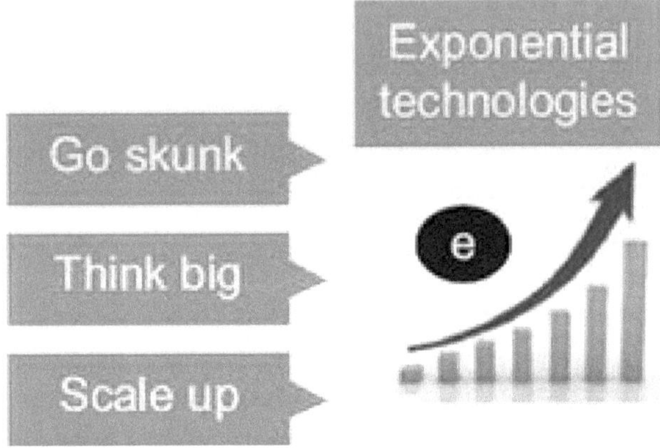

To survive and ultimately thrive in an exponential world, you need a mental toolkit for thinking at scale. That's the key to the billion-dollar opportunities of the future – being able to see what becomes not only feasible but also very desirable once exponential technologies come into play. Be prepared to go skunk, think big and scale up because the technology is coming which will make that possible.

GO SKUNK

In 1943, the US Department of Defense contacted Clarence "Kelly" Johnson, Lockheed's chief engineer, in a panic. German jet fighters had just appeared in the skies of Europe and America didn't have anything to respond with. Kelly assembled a group of his best engineers and sent them off to a rented circus tent which was located right next to a stinky plastics factory. The engineers started calling their secretive workplace the "skunkworks" and the term has stuck ever since.

Lockheed's engineers succeeded in delivering the United States's first military jet to the Pentagon just 143 days later — in less time than it normally takes the Army to approve paperwork to start building anything. What was the secret of their success? Lockheed's engineers were given an incredibly important mission, they had total design freedom and were completely walled off from the world. And that big goal — to save the world from Nazi peril — inspired Lockheed's engineers to move heaven and earth to deliver a crucial piece of military hardware in an impossibly short time frame.

You probably won't be on a mission to save the world but the simple reality is the skunk approach has worked for companies past and present. Apple used this approach to build the Macintosh. Google uses it today with its GoogleX project which is designed to let Google take moonshots that may or may not pay off. A skunkworks is the catalyst for innovation.

"In any organization, the bulk of your people will be climbing the hill they're standing on. That's what you want them to do. That's their job. A skunk works does a totally different job. It's a group of people looking for

a better hill to climb. This is threatening to the rest of the organization. It just makes good sense to separate these two groups."

– Astro Teller, manager, GoogleX

When a company sets up a skunkworks, it signals something interesting is in the air and it's not business as usual. A good skunkworks will act as an innovation accelerator. The three characteristics which make a skunkworks viable are:

1. *There needs to be isolation* – so organizational inertia is neutralized and also so the workers can have autonomy to act.
2. *You have to be going after an awe-inspiring goal* – which gives a worthwhile psychological boost to everyone involved. GoogleX, for example, goes after 10X improvements rather than 10 percent gains. That's an audacious goal.
3. *There must be a high tolerance for experimentation and failure* – with the idea that rapid iteration (fail fast and fail often) is usually the best way to move forward.

A good skunkworks program will increase motivation and performance so that flow – an optimal state of performance where everyone performs at their best – is triggered. A skunkworks will provide the environmental, psychological, social and creative triggers of flow. Simply put, when you run a great skunkworks program, you increase the odds that you will in fact generate flow.

"Failure isn't a badge of shame. It is a rite of passage."

– Tony Hseih, CEO, Zappos

"A start-up is simply a skunk works without the big company around it. The upside is there's no Borg to get sucked back into; the downside is you have no money."

– Astro Teller, manager, GoogleX

THINK BIG

There's no way around it – bold ideas are always big. To be bold, you've got to be prepared to have some massive dreams which create "super-credibility". To explain what this is, keep in mind that you already have a mental line of credibility.

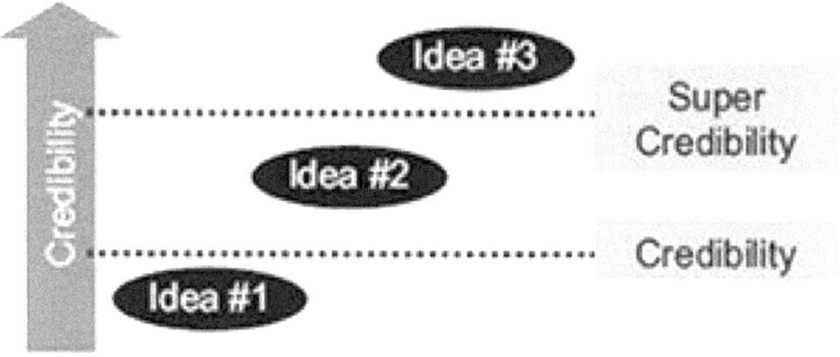

If someone pitches you an idea (idea #1) that is below your line of credibility, you will immediately dismiss it as ridiculous. If you place another idea (idea #2) above that line, you'll give it the benefit of the doubt and watch how it pans out. But there's also a line of super-credibility as well. When you hear a new idea which is above that line (idea #3), you will accept it and say, "Wow, that's fantastic! How can I get involved?" Big ideas can be so convincing your mind will immediately accept it as fact and instead of worrying about probabilities you start thinking about implications.

To be bold, you've got to have an idea which is above the threshold of super-credibility but which then gets broken down into bite-sized subgoals which just might be doable at a stretch. The more of those subgoals you achieve, the more believable your overall audacious goal will become. When you combine passion with a bold idea and achievable subgoals, you can achieve some pretty impressive things. It's all a matter of having the right mindset.

"Over the years I started collecting principles and truisms that have guided me in times of difficulty and opportunity. The maxims – "Peter's Laws" – are the ones that have worked for me, but that's no guarantee they will work for you. So come up with your own. Borrow from anyone you like. Start collecting mind hacks by examining your own life and seeing what worked."

– Peter Diamandis

PETER'S LAWS:

1. If anything can go wrong, fix it! (To hell with Murphy!)

2. When given a choice – take both!
3. Multiple projects lead to multiple successes.
4. Start at the top, then work your way up.
5. Do it by the book … but be the author!
6. When forced to compromise, ask for more.
7. If you can't win, change the rules.
8. If you can't change the rules, then ignore them.
9. Perfection is not optional.
10. When faced without a challenge – make one.
11. No simply means begin one level higher.
12. Don't walk when you can run.
13. When in doubt, THINK!
14. Patience is a virtue, but persistence to the point of success is a blessing.
15. The squeaky wheel gets replaced.
16. The faster you move, the slower time passes, the longer you live.
17. The best way to predict the future is to create it yourself.
18. The ratio of something to nothing is infinite.
19. You get what you incentivize.
20. If you think it is impossible, then it is for you.
21. An expert is someone who can tell you exactly how something can't be done.
22. The day before something is a breakthrough, it's a crazy idea.
23. If it was easy, it would be done already.
24. Without a target, you'll miss it every time.
25. Fail early, fail often, fail forward!

26. If you can't measure it, you can't improve it.
27. The world's most precious resource is the persistent and passionate human mind.
28. Bureaucracy is an obstacle to be conquered with persistence, confidence, and a bulldozer when necessary.

SCALE UP

When you look at successful entrepreneurs who build multi-billion-dollar companies which change the world, you'll notice that all of them have pursued bold ideas. Equally important, however, is the fact billionaires think and act at scale.

> *"Exponential technology allows us to scale up like never before. Small groups can have huge impacts. A team of passionate innovators can alter the lives of a billion people in an eye blink. To say that this kind of impact is unfathomable is putting it mildly."*
>
> *– Peter Diamandis and Steven Kotler*

Billionaires like Elon Musk, Richard Branson, Jeff Bezos and Larry Page all use the same eight mental strategies to think at scale:

1. Risk-taking and risk mitigation
2. Rapid iteration and ceaseless experimentation
3. Passion and purpose
4. Long-term thinking
5. Customer-centric thinking

6. Probabilistic thinking
7. Rationally optimistic thinking
8. Reliance on first principles aka fundamental truths

"I didn't go into the rocket business, the car business, or the solar business thinking this is a great opportunity. I just thought, in order to make a difference, something needed to be done. I wanted to have an impact. I wanted to create something substantially better than what came before."

– Elon Musk

"What's going to change in the next ten years?" And that is a very interesting question; it's a very common one. I almost never get the question: "What's not going to change in the next ten years?" And I submit to you that that second question is actually the more important of the two—because you can build a business strategy around the things that are stable in time."

– Jeff Bezos

"Unless you're customer-centric, you might be able to create something wonderful, but you're not going to survive. It's about getting every little detail right. It is running your airline like you would an upscale restaurant—the kind where the owner is there every day. Virgin Atlantic started out with one plane against

British Airways's hundred planes. On paper, we should not have survived. But because we were customer-centric, people went out of their way to fly us."

– Richard Branson

"The way I think about it, if you want to invent, if you want to do any innovation, anything new, you're going to have failures because you need to experiment. I think the amount of useful invention you do is directly proportional to the number of experiments you can run per week per month per year. So if you're going to increase the number of experiments, you're also going to increase the number of failures. And if you're going to invent, you've got to be willing to be misunderstood for long periods of time."

– Jeff Bezos

"We always try to concentrate on the long term. Many of the things we started—like Chrome—were seen as crazy when we launched them. So how do we decide what to do? How do we decide what's really important to work on? I like to call it the "toothbrush test." The toothbrush test is simple: Do you use it as often as you use your toothbrush? For most people, I guess that's twice a day. I think we really want things like that."

– Larry Page

"Position yourself with something that captures your curiosity, something that you're missionary about. I tell people that when we acquire companies, I'm always trying to figure out: Is this person who leads this company a missionary or a mercenary? The missionary is building the product and building the service because they love the customer, because they love the product, because they love the service. The mercenary is building the product or service so that they can flip the company and make money. One of the great paradoxes is that the missionaries end up making more money than the mercenaries anyway. And so pick something that you are passionate about, that's my number one piece of advice."

– Jeff Bezos

3. HOW TO JOIN THE BOLD CROWD

To leverage today's emerging exponential technologies and sell to today's hyper connected customers, there are four things you should be doing right now:

1. Start figuring out how you can use crowdsourcing to speed up your business
2. Run some incentive competitions to generate the breakthroughs you need
3. Learn how to make savvy use of crowdfunding to raise the capital you need

4. Build communities and use them to tackle big and bold challenges

1. START FIGURING OUT HOW YOU CAN USE CROWDSOURCING TO SPEED UP YOUR BUSINESS

Over the next decade, approximately 3 billion people will start using the Internet for the first time. This is due to more widespread communications technology which is becoming more affordable and more easily accessible. That means that the crowd is becoming hyper connected and hyper responsive to an extent never before seen in history.

As a direct consequence, crowdsourcing is flourishing. There are now some very powerful tools which are available to everyone and crowdsourcing companies are growing strongly. Some of the early leaders in this field are:

- Freelancer.com – 10 million users who took more than 5.4 million jobs generating $1.39 billion in revenues last year alone. Software companies are outsourcing their work to the cloud all the time.
- Tongal – a crowdsourcing platform which creates broadcast quality TV commercials ten times cheaper and ten times faster than standard processes.

You can now crowdsource all kinds of business tasks, access creative or operational assets, run testing and discovery projects and much more using nothing more than your credit card and a crowdsourcing service. The possibilities are limitless.

So how should you use crowdsourcing? The twelve best practices of crowdsourcing are:

1. *Do your research* – try looking for crowdsourced options for everything you need to get done. They are already there and do things cheaper and faster.
2. *Just get busy* – sign up, post a project and try it. Learn by doing. You'll even get interesting ideas from those who bid on your projects.
3. *Turn to the message boards* – and learn how to run projects using the advice of the experts. Every platform has a community you should leverage.
4. *Be specific* – the crowd won't understand the philosophy of your business. Make it easy for people to know exactly what you're trying to do.
5. *Prepare your data* – and be ready to provide the crowd with ready-to-go files.
6. *Qualify your workers* – give them some small pilot projects first and see how they perform. You can then get the best to complete the entire project.
7. *Keep roles clear, simple and specific* – tell people what exactly you're after. Don't make them guess.
8. *Communicate clearly in detail and often* – give lots of feedback quickly and concisely.

9. *Don't micromanage* – be open to new and different ways of thinking. They just might suggest something much better.
10. *Always go for quality first* – not just the bidder with the lowest price. It's well worth paying a little more to get the best workers.
11. *Prepare for the flood* – all the good ideas which people looking for work will suggest. This is one of the key advantages of crowdsourcing so use it.
12. *Be open to new working methodologies* – crowdsourcing may put you in touch with highly qualified people who want to work to novel schedules or requirements. Try it out and you may be pleasantly surprised to find a better way to get things done.

2. RUN SOME INCENTIVE COMPETITIONS TO GENERATE THE BREAKTHROUGHS YOU NEED

One of the most powerful mechanisms available to the exponential entrepreneur is to run incentive competitions. The concept is simple: you put up a winner-takes-all prize and then let people organize themselves to go after it.

Incentive competitions are incredibly powerful. They raise visibility and attract new ideas and financial backing for potential solutions. Sponsors and advertisers love incentive competitions like professional sports. Furthermore, incentive competitions cast a wide net and get loads of people working on them – which is exactly what you want.

The great thing about incentive competitions is you pay only the winner but you also get the ideas from the also-rans as well. This can create tremendous leverage and some impressive cross-platform solutions nobody had ever considered. If your prize is big enough, your competition can also seed the market and create demand for the solution when it becomes available. Incentive competitions win at all kinds of different levels.

Keep in mind, however, incentive competitions are not a panacea for every business challenge you have. They really only work if you have some clear objective in mind but don't yet understand how to get there. Competitions need to be in a field where there is a crowd of innovators and a small team is capable of solving the challenge. If you're going after something which is very capital intensive, a competition probably won't be a good fit. You will also need to be flexible about who owns the intellectual property generated by the competition and have very flexible time lines.

Keep in mind the big three motivators which will attract teams to compete in your incentive competition will generally be money, recognition and frustration with the status quo. You have to design your incentive competition so it will deliver on each of those key motivators. You also will want to specify a goal but leave the exact process as to how to achieve that goal open to the participants to decide.

The best practices for running an incentive competition for the crowd are:

1. *Identify the key issue or problem you want to solve* – and make sure you drill right down to the core. Clarify what the world will look like after the prize is won.
2. *Define your guidelines and metrics* – how you will measure when the finish line has been crossed. Clarify how progress will be measured.
3. *Get structured properly* – specify the name of the challenge, the prize purse, the duration of the competition, the format of a solution and who will own the intellectual property at the end of it.
4. *Polish your rules* – make sure they prevent cheating and have clear key indicators of progress. Estimate your costs to run, judge and promote the competition and see if there are cheaper options.
5. *Launch your competition* – and position it above the line of super-credibility. Create buzz by publicizing who is competing. Do a great launch which targets the right niches and communities.
6. *Operate your competition transparently* – have the resources you need to liaise with teams, handle legal requirements, generate ongoing publicity and so on. You'll also need a public face for your competition and a panel of judges as well. Make sure you have all the elements of highly successful incentive competitions.

7. *Finish strongly and leverage your competition* – determining the winner needs to be noncontroversial. You then want to have a major prize-giving ceremony to maximize your publicity. Make this as telegenic as feasible.

> *"Today's world is awash in data, and mining this treasure trove for useful tidbits can be worth billions of dollars. Tomorrow's world will be even more information packed. As we are entering an era of a trillion sensors and ubiquitous networks, we are going to be able to gather data about anything, anywhere, anytime we want. Incentive prizes provide exponential entrepreneurs with an incredibly efficient method to extract tremendous knowledge out of this bounty, providing an innovation acceleration engine unrivaled in history."*
>
> *– Peter Diamandis and Steven Kotler*

3. LEARN HOW TO MAKE SAVVY USE OF CROWDFUNDING TO RAISE THE CAPITAL YOU NEED

Raising the money required has always been one of the greatest barriers to starting a new business. That's changing thanks to crowdfunding. Millions of backers have already poured billions of dollars into start-ups through crowdfunding and this trend is going to rise exponentially. Experts predict the $15 billion raised in crowdfunding in 2015 will grow into at least $300 billion in the next few years as confidence in crowdfunding rises.

The great thing about crowdfunding is it provides social proof of market demand. It also allows an entrepreneur to get started and build momentum. You can fund and launch a project at the same time using crowdfunding which is enormously helpful. There are already more than 700 crowdfunding websites online today and that number is expected to double over the next few years.

The four main types of crowdfunding are:

1. *Donation* – you give a worthy cause money and expect nothing in return.
2. *Debt* – you provide funds which will be repaid with interest.
3. *Equity* – you ask investors for cash in return for stock in your company.
4. *Reward or incentive* – the funder provides money to support the creation of some product or service they intend to use themselves or which inspires them.

As a rule-of-thumb donation funding tends to work for social causes and political campaigns. Debt funding is considered best for local projects which benefit a community. Equity funding is the new kid on the block and it's still a bit too early to see how crowdfunding for equity pans out in practice. Reward or incentive crowdfunding now has a decent entrepreneurial track record of success and has proven to be highly effective for both creative projects and actual products. So for now at least, most entrepreneurial ventures will probably go with the reward or incentive approach to crowdfunding.

For all its obvious allure, crowdfunding isn't for everyone. The best crowdfunding campaigns tend to have these key characteristics:

- The product is in late prototype stage and can be shown in action.
- You have a good management team in place so people can be confident something will happen with the money.
- The product is community based and consumer facing – it's something potential investors will buy and use themselves.
- The management team have a network of potential investors they can pitch to.
- The product aims to solve a compelling problem.

From your perspective, crowdfunding will provide market validation and real demand measurement. A good crowdfunding campaign will hopefully see a community of paying customers emerge which you can then sell to at low cost-per-customer acquisition costs. There are also obvious PR benefits as well. Crowdfunding tends to work best if you're completely passionate about your product and just want to get it out there quickly.

The twelve steps involved in running a good crowdfunding campaign are:

1. *Choose your ideal idea* – which will lie at the junction of something you're passionate about and something others will care about as well. Ask your community for ideas about what's needed.
2. *Set your crowdfunding target* – decide how much you will raise. To a large extent, this will be a function of what kinds of incentives you can offer funders. You also want to crowdfund to raise some of your development costs but not all. You have to show you have some skin in the game to be credible. Raise enough money that you can move forward but not so much that you make a killing. Also have some stretch goals in mind that describe things you can do if more people become involved.
3. *Set your campaign length and create a schedule* – typically 30- to 120-days. Generally, shorter campaigns work best. You then schedule what you will do during that window to build momentum. People love to back winners.
4. *Specify your incentives and your stretch goals* – what backers will get for contributing. Most campaigns tend to have $25, $50, $100, $500 and $1,000 level incentives with the $25 perk generating 25%of the responses. Offer something valuable and unique which can't be purchased elsewhere.

5. *Build the perfect execution team* – a celebrity (or face), a campaign manager / strategist, an expert, a graphic design guru and a technology manager. You can also add in PR manager and a super-connector if you have them.

6. *Prepare thoroughly* – get the materials and resources you'll need in place before you start your campaign, not after the initial rush has died down.

7. *Tell a meaningful story* – have a powerful, compelling narrative about why your product will be the best thing since sliced bread. Focus on the why this is needed more than the what.

8. *Create a viral video* – which brings your product to life and which puts faces to your ideas. Campaigns with short videos typically raise 239 percent more money than campaigns without a video.

9. *Build your audience* – with affiliates, advocates and activists leading the way. Make it clear you're embarking on a cause rather than just selling another widget.

10. *Launch your campaign properly* – come out of the gate with sizzle. Engage your early donors and hype things up. The first few days after you launch is when you gain traction and raise the most money so make it happen. Go for super-credibility.

11. *Keep engaging week after week* – stay in touch with everyone and let them know how you're doing. Provide status updates and ask backers to invite their friends.

Look for opportunities to do upsells at the same time. Keep your campaign in the news with promotions and contests.

12. *Make data-driven decisions* – about when to scale up, when to engage and when to jump on rising trends. Consider investing in Facebook, YouTube and LinkedIn advertising if the ads work.

4. BUILD COMMUNITIES AND USE THEM TO TACKLE BIG AND BOLD CHALLENGES

Your chances of doing something bold increase significantly if you build an exponential community you can tap into and work with. Today's online communities can tackle jobs which are impressive in scale and scope. A community today can tackle the kind of projects which previously were the exclusive province of large corporations or governments.

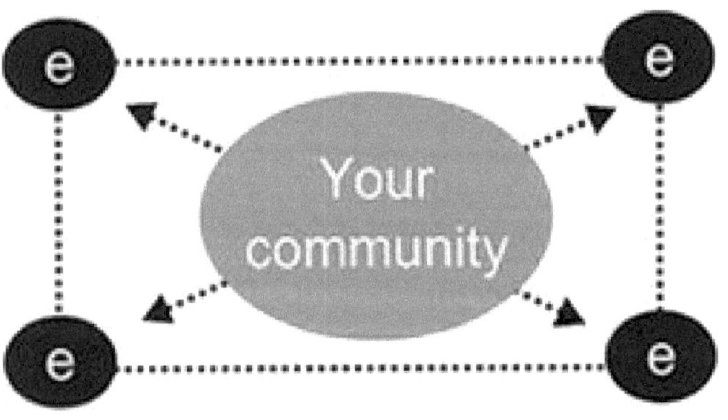

The great thing about communities is they can be self-organizing. They're built on reputation economics rather than financial exchanges. Simply put, people like to do things that impress their peers and enhance their personal reputations. If you build a community which is tackling an important task and then provide opportunities for individuals to shine within that community, you'll be amazed at the energy and creativity which get unleashed.

One of the most telling features of the web is what can be termed "The Law of Niches". No matter what oddball thing you're passionate about, there are plenty of folks who share your passion. Communities are a way to find others and to create a platform which will serve your needs. You can then leverage that community to build a business if you so choose or to tackle some big and bold challenges which society faces.

Building a vibrant exponential community usually involves eight key steps or stages of development:

1. *You define your massively transformative process –* what you're trying to achieve as a community and how you aspire to move the needle and make a difference. Tell your engaging story.
2. *Build your community portal –* something authentic which allows simple registration and two-way flow of information.

3. *Start recruiting members* – handpick your pioneers and then have some kind of newcomer's ritual which helps people feel like they belong.

4. *Create some community content* – in the form of an event, upcoming product launch, newsletters, online magazines, interviews, etc.

5. *Apply engagement strategies* – so as to get people to connect in ways that generate real emotions. You might have a talent leaderboard, run some real world meet-ups, or undertake challenges that require collaboration to enhance engagement.

6. *Actively manage your community* – by acting like a benign dictator. Communities are inherently messy so you'll need to keep things heading in the right direction and weed out distractions.

7. *Continue to grow your community* – by expanding opportunities for people to talk with each other and through evangelism. Picking a fight with some other entity or running some awe-inspiring competitions are also great community growth strategies.

8. *Monetize your community* – which will be feasible as long as you are transparent and authentic in how you do this. The best way to monetize is to sell what the community builds and share the spoils with the community. You can also sell ads and premium memberships as long as you take care to cater to your core at the same time.

Communities of believers can be a great asset and the perfect way to be bold. Build your community now and prosper as you undertake bold projects.

Get the main ideas of this book in less than 30 minutes

Buy the books you really need thanks to our must-read summaries!

Available on all devices

www.mustreadsummaries.com